FROM WAVES, I RISE

FROM WAVES, I RISE

A COLLECTION OF POEMS

NIHARIKA GHOSH

NEW DEGREE PRESS

FROM WAVES, I RISE

A Collection of Poems

ISBN   978-1-63730-368-9 *Paperback*

            978-1-63730-369-6 *Kindle Ebook*

            978-1-63730-370-2 *Ebook*

To Riya

my sister, soul mate, and best friend

CONTENTS

AUTHOR'S NOTE

I began writing poetry because I was lost. Lost in my own head, lost in the world, and lost trying to find myself while navigating the waters of teenage life: family and friendship, relationships, and mental illness. I found solace by writing, turning the chaos in my mind into words on a page. My poems became my safe haven—a way for me to reflect upon myself and the world around me, depict my emotions through art, and remind myself about the beautiful things in life.

This collection was originally titled "Before 18" because all the poems were written in the span of one year, when I was seventeen years old. These poems touch on hard subjects—such as mental illness, trauma, and loss—inspired by my personal experiences in my last year before adulthood. Writing poetry was my way of coping with my sometimes-overwhelming emotions, and I wanted to share these poems and my journey with the world. My hope is that, in reading this book, you will be moved emotionally and feel personally connected to the poems. I want you to see this book as an opportunity to reflect upon yourself and your experiences, and if you have shared these feelings before, to embrace them. Everyone has gone through mental challenges and conflict of some kind—which often leave a lasting impact on one's mental health. It is important for all of us to learn self-love, compassion and how to confront uncomfortable feelings so that we may heal. Healing is a painful, messy process, but it is possible. I want to leave you with a sense of hope as you close the last page.

From Waves, I Rise is written in five parts:

Part I: Nature—This section focuses on the beauty of nature and its power to energize and empower the mind. These poems will draw you into the tranquility and peacefulness of nature around us and provide an escape from the chaos of daily life.

Part II: Childhood—This section explores the themes of growing up and leaving childhood behind as one emerges into the turbulent state between childhood and adulthood.

Part III: Hurting—These poems focus on the experiences of mental health issues, trauma, and facing difficult challenges, including self-image, depression, anxiety, sexual assault, and substance abuse.

Part IV: The Dark Side of Loving—This section explores the passionate and volatile nature of young love and the heartbreak, pain, and suffering that comes along with it.

Part V: Healing—These poems offer a message of inspiration about healing from the past. By exploring self-compassion and growth, these poems empower the reader to grow from their experiences and look towards the future with hope.

You will love this collection if you enjoy reading emotional poetry, have dealt with mental health issues, or want to focus on learning how to heal from the past. Most importantly, you will love this book if you have been a teenager yourself, because everyone shares the rollercoaster journey of ups and downs experienced during these transformative years. Ultimately, I hope that my poems inspire reflection and fruitful dialogue, pressing into engaging questions such as:

How can I confront and heal from my own trauma?

How can I have a stronger emotional understanding of my loved ones?

How do these themes relate to the larger mental health crisis in society?

I look forward to exploring these questions and beyond with my readers. I believe discussing trauma, pain, and healing will change us all for the better. This collection is meant to be empowering and uplifting, sharing the message that it is okay to make mistakes and go through hardships, but knowing that at the end of the day you are never alone. You still have the power and strength within you to heal and find happiness. I hope that you—as the reader—will embrace this mentality, so that together—from the darkness, from the waves—we can rise.

Life is a journey of hurting and healing,
just as the sun rises and falls every day.
But the sun will always rise again.

NIHARIKA GHOSH

NATURE

~

the nature of freedom

as i stand in
the silence of nature
my heart
beats in my ears
and the last golden touch
of sunlight caresses the treetops

i forget
the clash and chaos
constant movement
of life

here,
amidst the pines
the birds hear my words
and answer back in song
the squirrels fly above my head
in their endless games of chase
and the trees bow
to protect me
wherever my path may lead

here,
submerged in unfiltered light
i am hidden
i am lost
i am free

children of the sun

I.
imagine a world
where we are not children of the sun
but children of the moon

our eyes would glimmer
with the depth of night
instead of sparkling in the sun

the heat of the day
would be our blanket:
warming us as
we peacefully slumbered

we would rise when
the world became dark
and dance beneath the stars

II.
what if we were children of the moon?
worshippers of the night
embracing all it reveals
about the true nature of light:

how when it is scarce
we treasure it all the more

battle cry

you've heard nature's battle cry
in the roar of the wind,
the creak of the trees
as she pleads for the lives of her children

every oil-ridden lake
every cloud of smoke
makes her cry stronger

every lost life
is a burning tree
in a forest of flames

but i tell her that the phoenix
rises from its own ashes

as the leaves turn to dust and
float
      to
          the
               ground

i open my arms to
a new beginning:
one where we are reborn
from our mother's remains

dancing flames

does fire
bring life, or death?

do flames eat away at wood—
turning it to ash—
or do they help something new
break free?

the flames hiss to me—
memories of the beating wind—
as they release
smoky spirits into the sky,

working tirelessly
to consume every
stick, every log

i merely watch them lick the air
entrapped by their endless dance

through the woods

on a walk through the woods
at sunset,
the light slices through the air,
bathes the trees in gold

a wooden bridge,
a circle of stumps,
a crumbling stone wall—
signs of human life
peppered throughout the wilderness

deeper and deeper i go
paths turned to beds of leaves
and limbs tower over me,
rusty colors swaying in the wind;

each step brings me closer
to the crest of the hill
until at last—i stand upon
a mossy rock

closing my eyes—i turn to face
the heat of fading day
autumnal air fills my lungs as
i fall back:
back to the earth,
back to reality,
back to the gray of life
where the sun's golden rays
are smothered by smoke

spring

i can already feel it:
the smallest hint of change
passing through the air

the sky is brighter
the days longer
and the sun goes off to slumber much later

a brief moment of warmth
courses through the biting cold
teasing you with laughter

though the trees are bare
and the night still ice
i feel it coming:
spring is near

butterfly

butterfly, butterfly
lift me away
on your colored wings

how freely you fly
from flower to flower
drinking ambrosia and nectar

with envy i watch you flutter
as i am trapped
in this lonely prison

take me away, butterfly
bring me to the skies
fly me to your paradise

CHILDHOOD

~

mermaids

I.
when we were kids we
pretended that we
were mermaids;
the pool became the ocean,
we created our own world
at our fingertips

but when people ask,
i say i have no stories of childhood;
everyone knows mermaids
are merely dreams

II.
inside my mind
i travel
to magical realms where
mermaids sing;
where i can't hear the screams

III.
back then my
mind was free
from the choking grip of itself
i was a girl that just wanted
to be a mermaid;
but she drowned

IV.
waves turned to tsunamis
and now i am nothing but
a skeleton
of a girl who once dreamed
about mermaids

balloons

a thousand balloons
        i shall tie to my hand
until my feet are
        lifted off the ground
blood drips down
        my wrist as the strings cut deep—
but i hold on tight

for at least the sky
        will welcome me

first snow

outside frosted windows i see
the first snow of the year
a world of green turned white
as the magic returns

on a nearby hill
children scream
with delight as they fly
on colorful sleds

in a field
a young one builds
a companion of snow
with stone eyes and mouth

i close my eyes and fall back
onto the bed of snow,
let my mind take over
as the cold consumes my body

i turn back and see
my creation: an angel on earth,
another testament to the
magic of winter

sweet insomniac

sleep now,
let the darkness
wrap you in her arms
you are safe now

gone are your troubles and fears
your anxiety
your regrets
let them melt away

with heavy weights upon your eyes
release yourself to slumber
faraway lands call to you
with intoxicating lullabies

sleep now, my dear
let the darkness
cradle you in her warmth
she will keep you safe

jumping off

in my dreams—where time is warped—
i decide to jump off the ship
i dive into the cerulean sea,
    entering another realm

invisible hands try to pull me back
desperately trying to keep me tethered
to the mast and its faceless ideals:
standards i will never meet

but i thrash and kick
in the blue abyss
until at last i can breathe
until at last i can accept myself

grief

i grieve
the death of my childhood

i bury the girl who read books in blanket forts
and sang in public without fear

i cremate my innocence
along with my dreams

from the ashes a new me is born
i try to not envy my remains

hands

my hands were soft
upon my mother's chest
tiny and innocent
and loved beyond compare

i learned to love
the dirt under my fingernails
the palms that grasped my father's
as he swung me in circles
the fingers that intertwined with my mother's
as we walked to school

my hands turned paper into planes
flowers into crowns
dreams into reality

then—my hands learned
the touch of a lover
now hands were not
tools for creation
but bridges connecting him to me

these hands have endured a lifetime
are practiced at stifling laughter
at wiping away tears

and one day
these hands shall
lay upon my chest
as i close my eyes and fade away
may they be as useful
in the next life as they were
in this one

HURTING

~

a crowded hallway

eyes cast down
she walks
one step
then another

she ignores
the burning stares
the harsh whispers
the not-so-gentle shoves

keep going,
she says
just another second
another minute
another hour
almost there

but just as safety
is a breath away
it dissolves into darkness

she finds herself
at the start
of another crowded hallway

wave

the wave rises within her—
growing,
swelling—
it is seconds away
from collapsing

but she fights to keep it contained:
the tears, the screams
that threaten to rip her
in half

her poisoned brain
waits, yearns to become one
with the water,
to drown out the world

what is one more tear
when a wave
is destined to crash?

broken mirrors

broken glass and shattered mirrors
my face split into a thousand pieces
a thousand eyes searching for
the fragmented parts of my soul

staring harder now, i find
the face i used to know
but she fades and splits apart
just as lightning breaks the sky

waterfall

it amazes me
how clearly i can speak
through a waterfall of tears;
i can't seem to remember
the moment when
i learned to cry so quietly
that the world would never hear

you hear my voice but fail to see
how every word brings back
years of hurt and pain and loss
i learned to be quiet
i learned that you would not listen
i learned that you did not care

even though my screams
echoed in the chasm between us
i turned away, hiding
my tears behind
the waterfall

buzzing thoughts

swarms of flies
buzz between my ears

thoughts rush like rapids
faster, faster, stronger, churning

the pressure builds until i am a
a balloon too full of air

i know someday i will

pop

it's fine

"it's fine—i'm clean!"
i said as i ran past my mother's arms
tracking mud into the house

running
            running
                        running

"it's fine—i'm clean!"
he said as he ran past
my protests

"no, please, no..."
i repeated
i begged

"but it's fine," you said
so i just closed my eyes

and told myself
everything's fine

shower

the hot water washes
away your marks
i feel them lift off my skin
like a cloud,
until all that is left underneath
are the scars i am familiar with

i scrub until i reveal skin
that your fingers did not touch
until my body doesn't remember
your grip, the marks you left

and i am born again—
a new flame, prepared to
forgive the darkness,
to cast my light upon others
who seek it

smoke

inhale
> it consumes me
> reaches into my body,
> fills every vein

exhale
> from the corners of my mouth
> a cloud forms
> curls up to the sky

inhale
> heavenly perfume
> rushes to my head
> lifts me to another
> world, another dimension
> i never want to come down

exhale
> the cycle repeats
> once you enter the smoke
> you can never leave it

inhale

unravel

how i wish
to go back in time
and unravel the events of my past

unwind the spool
and cut the thread
where everything went wrong

when gossamer string turned
to knots and tangles
a web of secrets and lies

how i wish i could erase
the mistakes that altered my life

but alas this string
keeps tangling
knotting itself against time

i suppose only fate—
with her shiny shears—
will decide when it will break

THE DARK SIDE
OF LOVING

my sun

i used to think
you were the sun
the center of my universe

my world revolved
around you
my life ensnared in your orbit

but your fire grew
and became overwhelming
only too late did i see
how you suffocated me

i believed with all my heart
that you were my sun
little did i know
the sun is blinding

pedestal

i crafted you myself
a grand statue of marble—
my idol, my muse,
the image of perfection—
and placed you high above

while i knelt at your feet
believing myself only worthy
to remain at that level
yet, there were cracks within your stone

i should have seen
you were nothing more
than a skeleton
of who i believed you to be

and it should have been me
on that pedestal
with you bowing
upon the ground

young love

the warm smells of her body
fill my nose: vanilla, rose, lavender...

her skin pressed against mine
i feel her sweat mix with my own desire

though we both struggle to breathe
i find comfort in our proximity

we are closer than we have ever been
than we will ever be

first breath

deeper i sink
into the comforting darkness
and numbing cold
a bed of ice and sand,

but water will only
dull your senses for so long
before you must come up for air
emerge into the light again

and in that moment
you were my breath
when i didn't even know
i was drowning

sweetness

i didn't think i was special
maybe that's why i let you
convince me that i was

your words were like honey:
i should have known they were
too sweet to be true

but i grew hungry for more,
this butterfly turned beast
as i hunted for my next fix

i sought another love,
with more tender hands
more tender words

but soon i became drunk
off my own sweetness

i found myself surrounded by bees—
ready to sting me to win back
the love that was not
mine to take in the first place

i was alone once more
with not even you by my side
maybe
                    i wasn't so special
                            after all

lust or love

was it lust or love?
when he brought me to his car
and offered me a kiss
said how beautiful i was

was it lust or love?
when he took me by the hand
and brought me to the dark
to touch my body

was it lust or love?
when he told me that he loved me
and if i loved him back
i had to pleasure him

was it lust or love?
when he bruised me with his kisses
saying only that he needed
to show who i belonged to

but really, if he loved me
would he have stolen my heart
and left me with broken pieces?
how could that be love?

beautiful

you called me beautiful
traced my body
with your paintbrush fingers
skin on skin
a stranger's touch
a devil in sheep's clothing

"such beautiful skin,"
you wrapped your hand around my neck
the other gripped my thigh

"such beautiful lips,"
you devoured them

but if i was so beautiful
why did you leave me
ashamed and alone
covered in bruises and scars

am i still beautiful now

diamond

you treat me like dirt
but really i am
a diamond
unborn

i wait beneath the soil
under your feet
though you attempt
to bury me
i will endure

for years i wait
withstanding unbelievable pressure
growing stronger
as you wither away

until at last
i emerge as the gem
you never could see
inside of me

hidden scars

your hands are swords
and your eyes are bullets
we dance in circles
to see who will fall first

knives draw on my body as
you bark your words like thunder
throw boulders
upon my chest

but after all is said and done
these words will melt away
and i will still be here
standing strong

HEALING

~

ripples

let this be a reminder:

we are not glass
    broken once dropped

we are not ice
    melting away in light

we are water
    we come back together when
    a stone is thrown

we heal after we are broken

stormy sea

it was like jumping off a boat
in an angry storm
i tried to hold on
but the waves were ruthless,
the rain never-ending

the waves crested,
i faced a wall of water,
took a deep breath
and dove under the surface

suddenly everything was calm
the thunder hushed
the dark waters reflected
the smiling stars

and i floated by myself
i didn't need a boat after all
i only needed to trust myself

piano

as my fingers rest upon
the ivory petals,

i hear
a voice calling
surrounding me with
sweet drops of song

the melody flows
through my ears to
my fingers, as if i were
possessed by the ghost
of music

each note rings clear:
melody and harmony
birthing a lamenting tune
intertwining with my thoughts

i close my eyes
as the song consumes me
until the piano and i
flow together as
one

painting

as i dip my brush into the water
i feel something greater take over

it is no longer just a brush
but an extension of my hand
waiting to turn my energy
into a story upon the page

a drop of color blossoms into a flower
and a wave crashes on canvas
the scene unfolds
with a vitality and life of its own

this painting is no longer
a figment of my imagination
but an entirely new world
for my mind to dive into
to be lost
before i find it again

thunder and lightning

i am like a bucket brimming
just one more drop
and then comes the flood

the words keep building,
pushing against my throat
but my mouth is a dam—
one day it will break

silence me now
but

just as thunder
follows lightning
i will speak,
set fire to your world

and from the ashes
i rise, reborn
a new flame

letting go

rest your head
in the crook of your elbow
feel the sunlight
caress your face
lose yourself in
a bird's song

cherish this moment,
this peace
let your mind wander
let go

of your regrets
of your anxiety
of everything holding you back

feel the sunlight
caress your face
and let the world
fall away

one day at a time

every day
you take a step further
along this
path of life

every decision
every choice
has led you
to where you now stand

why spend your days
living in the past?
why poison your mind,
falling ill to regret?

every day
you are one step further
with every laugh—every smile—
a part of you is healed

the small joys in life

waking up to catch the sunrise
wearing a sweater fresh out the dryer
the smell of freshly washed hair
running through sprinklers on a hot summer day
blowing out candles on a cake
screaming songs in the shower
diving into ocean waves
sitting by the fireplace
hearing a song that gives you chills
catching snowflakes on your tongue
a clear night full of stars

these are the small things
that make life worth living

desert

i am like the desert
constantly shifting
   moving
   blowing
   changing,
never the same for too long

my sands have blown
across the world
they shape the land
around me

as the winds blow
i am a storm of dust
rising and growing
consuming the earth
until at last i settle again
and i am a waterless ocean

life lessons

at the end of the day,
what is life really?
to walk through the darkness
to see the joy of light
to feel fire burning through your body
to hurt and scream and cry
tears of laughter—
sometimes we must die first
before we can truly live

a new dawn

many suns have come and gone
and still here we stand—
through winter, spring, summer, and fall
and winter once more—
behind screens and behind walls
yet together through it all

a new age,
a new dawn rises
change is in the air

history

we cannot rewrite history
there is no use wondering
what could have gone differently
all of this, no matter how unpleasant,
has already happened
so why waste your energy
wishing to go back?

we can write our own stories
we can write our own future—
that which is not yet set in stone—
so with every step forward
you get to carve your own path
into the unknown

you will stumble
sometimes fall
but your scrapes will be healed
time will turn them into beautiful scars:
reminders of your past
mistakes you will not make again

time moves forward
and so will you
and with a strong heart and steady mind
you shall create your own history

ACKNOWLEDGMENTS

You never know how much work it will take to reach your final destination when setting out on a long journey you have not embarked on before. I have discovered—along my journey writing *From Waves, I Rise*—that publishing a book takes a village, and I am so grateful for all the support. Fulfilling this dream would not have been possible without you.

Thank you first and foremost to my family for supporting me through every step of the way and for always helping me up when I stumble or face obstacles. Thank you Sonamama and Bapi for being the most incredible parents. I really would not have been able to do this without your unconditional love and support. I draw my strength, determination, and passion for art from you. Thank you Dadu, Dida, Mamma, and Babuji for always being my number one fans. Thank you Megh for being the older sister I never had and always encouraging me when I felt doubtful about myself. And most importantly, thank you Riya for being by my side when I was at my lowest. You are the light that guides me when I get trapped in the darkness. I love you all.

Thank you, Professor Eric Koester, for providing me with the opportunity to publish my first book through the Book Creators program. Thank you to my editors—Melody Delgado Lorbeer, Tasslyn Magnusson, and Kristin Gustafson—for turning my collection into a masterpiece. Thank you Gjorgji Pejkovski, Ana Jovanovska and the Creative Design team for helping design my book cover. Thank you to Brian Bies and everyone at New Degree Press for providing the necessary resources for publishing this book. I am beyond grateful for all your help and guidance throughout the writing and publishing process.

To everyone who donated to my campaign and preordered my book, thank you for helping me during the early stages of this journey. Thank you Ashavari Baral, Boyang Wang, Sherry You, Briana Yang, Vivian Zander, Juliet Jiang, Olivia Gaston, Kelly Rosendo, Bill Wu, Henry Madden, Katherine Zeng, Carlie Caperan, Sophie Wilson, Emma Southard, Isabella Balian, Georgia Lawrence, Elysia Yuan, Danielle Rabe, Brooke McGurl, Grace Carlisle, McKenna McDaniels, Adriana Garber, Leo Wang, Owen Davies, Rituparna Chatterjee, Shubhodeep Basu, Vidhi Chhaochharia, Suman Ghosh, Soumendra Nanda, Ajoy & Bina Ghosh, Kamales & Aparna Nanda, Tania Dutta, Tanya Rahman, Malini Gupta, Beena Chatterjee, Arpita Bhattacharjee, Urmi Purakayastha, Koushik Chakrabarty, Shayantan Mukherjee, Joel Buford, Zachary Pava, Chris Kurhajetz, Jessica Eaton, Erika Guckenberger, Susan Shane, Joanna Colton, Vicki Vanderschmidt, Katie Bettencourt, Prim Sawyer, Karen Garber, Laura McAnena, Paramita Sen, Pragati Bhowmick, Nifemi Aluko, Sourav Ganguly, Anita Ajmiri, Kavita Parwani Talib, Arup Dey, Vrishab Sikand, Emanuele Bianchini, Alyssa Pierce, Shamir

L, Patrick Frank, Shannon Ericson, Melanie Singer, Kamakshi Raman, Shashikala Raj, Mausumi Dey, Ruhul Abid, Swati Chandra, Made Jalan, Melissa Statires, Pubali Banerjee, Allyson Hayden, Dipanwita Bhattacharyya, Kristine Kamikawa, Soumi Mukhopadhyay, Jamie Bosse, Carlo Mahfouz, Sonali Basu Parekh, Hannah Nyren, Maura Sullivan, Elizabeth Sinoff, Bashu Baksi, Anindya Chatterjee, Colette Tracy, Terri Nakamura, Saumyadipta Nanda, Siddhartha & Sanghamitra Bhattacharya, Parbati Bhattacharya, Susmita Sen, Arun & Nina Bhattacharjee, Shahana Bhattacharya, Shohini Bhattacharya, Sarmishtha Mukherjee, Sunil Mukherjee, Gora Nanda, Sukanya Chatterjee, Chetna Kumar, Nilanjana Bhattacharya, Sumon & Seema Mazumdar, Shuvayu & Swati Kanjilal, Paramita Das & Sambit Basu, Sashi Raj, Shilpa Thomas, Poorti Marino, Shauli Manas, Ishana Deb, Lisa Stuart, Lisa Sinoff and everyone else for their words of encouragement throughout the whole process.

I extend my heartfelt gratitude to every single one of you for supporting me. Thank you for being a part of my journey and turning one of my lifelong dreams into a reality.